On the Path Home

Library of Congress Cataloging-in-Publication Data
Names: Eyring, Henry B., 1933–   author.
Title: On the path home / Henry B. Eyring.
Description: Salt Lake City, Utah : Deseret Book, [2016] | Includes bibliographical
   references.
Identifiers: LCCN 2016012643 | ISBN 9781629722535 (hardbound : alk. paper)
Subjects: LCSH: Mormons—Conduct of life. | Mormons—Religious life. | Christian life—
   Mormon authors.
Classification: LCC BX8656 .E9575 2016 | DDC 248.4/89332—dc23
LC record available at https://lccn.loc.gov/2016012643

Printed in China
RR Donnelley, Shenzhen, China

10   9   8   7   6   5   4   3   2   1

On the Path Home

HENRY B. EYRING

DESERET
BOOK

Salt Lake City, Utah

Every person is different and has a
different contribution to make.

No one is destined to fail.

For each of us, life is a

Heavenly Father designed it for us out of love. Each of us has unique experiences and characteristics, but our journey began in the same place before we were born into this world.

We need STRENGTH BEYOND OURSELVES to keep the commandments in whatever circumstance life brings to us. The combination of trials and their duration are as varied as are the children of our Heavenly Father. No two are alike.

But what is being tested is the same, at all times in our lives and for every person: WILL WE DO WHATSOEVER THE LORD OUR GOD WILL COMMAND US?

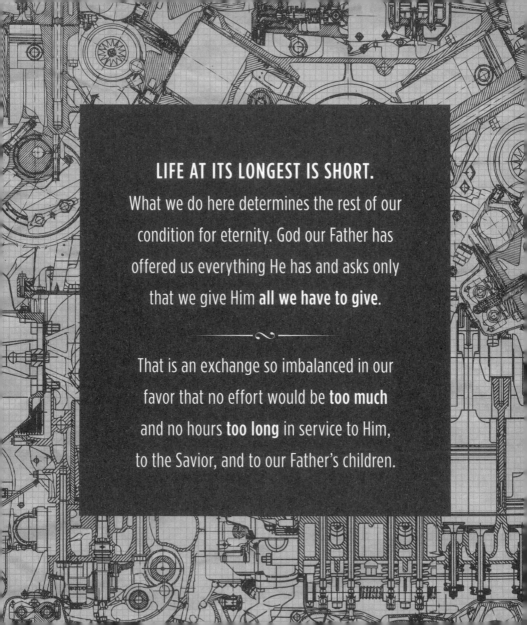

LIFE AT ITS LONGEST IS SHORT.

What we do here determines the rest of our condition for eternity. God our Father has offered us everything He has and asks only that we give Him **all we have to give**.

———— ∽ ————

That is an exchange so imbalanced in our favor that no effort would be **too much** and no hours **too long** in service to Him, to the Savior, and to our Father's children.

TIME is the property we inherit from God, along with the power to **CHOOSE** what we will do with it.

Whoever you are and wherever you may be, you hold in your hands the **HAPPINESS** of more people than you can now imagine.

When you choose
whether to make or keep
a covenant with God, you
choose whether you will
leave an inheritance of

to those who might
follow your example.

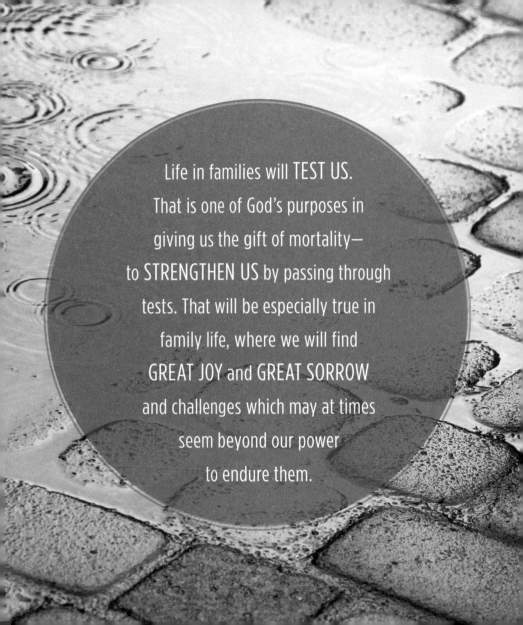

Life in families will TEST US.
That is one of God's purposes in
giving us the gift of mortality—
to STRENGTHEN US by passing through
tests. That will be especially true in
family life, where we will find
GREAT JOY and GREAT SORROW
and challenges which may at times
seem beyond our power
to endure them.

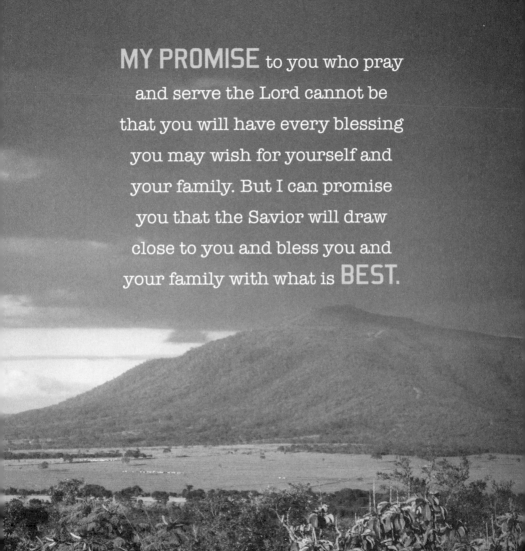

MY PROMISE to you who pray and serve the Lord cannot be that you will have every blessing you may wish for yourself and your family. But I can promise you that the Savior will draw close to you and bless you and your family with what is BEST.

The Holy Ghost is sent to
you and to those you care for.
You will be strengthened and
yet inspired to know the limits
and extent of your ability to
serve. The Spirit will comfort
you when you may wonder,
"DID I DO ENOUGH?"

The Savior not only understands
and feels grief but also feels your

PERSONAL GRIEF that only you

feel. And He knows you perfectly.

HE KNOWS YOUR HEART.

So He can know which of the many

things you can do that will be best

for you as you invite the Holy Ghost

to comfort and bless you.

The Lord knows both what He will need you to **DO** and what you will need to **KNOW.** He is kind and He is all-knowing.

So you can with confidence expect that He has **PREPARED** opportunities for you to learn in preparation for the **SERVICE** you will give.

It will take UNSHAKABLE FAITH in the Lord
Jesus Christ to choose the way to eternal life.
When tragedy strikes or even when it looms,
our families will have the opportunity to
LOOK INTO OUR HEARTS to see whether we
know what we said we knew. Our children will
watch, feel the Spirit confirm that we lived as
we preached, remember that confirmation,
and pass the story across the generations.

Human judgment and logical thinking will not be enough to get answers to the questions that matter most in life. We need REVELATION from God.

Just as pondering the scriptures invites the companionship of the Holy Ghost, so does doing the things we have been told to do and doing them PROMPTLY. We are promised that the scriptures and the Holy Ghost will tell us all things that we should do.

When we go and do what we have been told and do it the best we can, we QUALIFY for MORE INSTRUCTIONS of what to do.

EVERY COVENANT
with God is an opportunity
to DRAW CLOSER
to Him. To anyone who
reflects for a moment
on what they have
already felt of the love of
God, to have that bond
made stronger and that
relationship closer is an
IRRESISTIBLE offer.

If you are on the **RIGHT PATH,**
it will always be **UPHILL.**

The Lord is anxious
to lead us to the safety
of **HIGHER GROUND.**

Heavenly Father has assigned us
to a great variety of stations to
strengthen and, when needed, to
LEAD TRAVELERS TO SAFETY.

Our most important and powerful
assignments are in the family.
They are important because the
family has the opportunity at the
start of a child's life to put feet
firmly on the PATH HOME.

A CLEAR LIGHT

piercing the darkness

will show the way to

those who have taken the

Holy Ghost as a trusted

and constant traveling

COMPANION.

E

N N

F N

X Z

D T F

N P T H

N T D Z

T Z F H

Among the reasons we ought to be thankful is that it will improve our **VISION.** And with an eye on today's blessings you'll have more staying power for the distant goal.

20 ft
6.1 m

15 ft
4.6 m

Let us do whatever is required to
qualify for the Holy Ghost as
our companion, and then let us
go forward fearlessly so that we
will be given the powers to do
whatever the Lord calls us to do.

That growth in power to serve
may come slowly, it may come in
small steps that are difficult for you
to see, BUT IT WILL COME.

Each time a LINE OF TRUTH comes to us,
we get to choose what we will do about it.
If we try hard to do what that truth requires
of us, God will send MORE LIGHT and
more truth. It will go on, line after line, as
long as we choose to obey the truth.

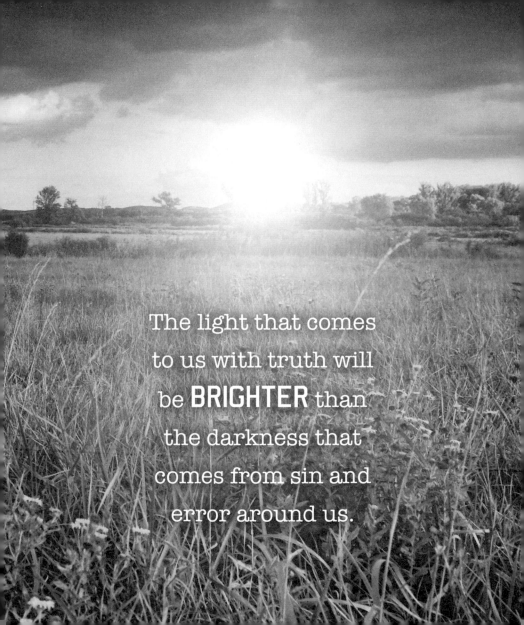

The light that comes
to us with truth will
be **BRIGHTER** than
the darkness that
comes from sin and
error around us.

The great test of life
is to see whether we
will hearken to and
obey God's commands
in the midst of the
STORMS OF LIFE.
It is not to endure
storms, but to choose
the right while they
RAGE.

After all we can do in faith,

the Lord will justify our hopes for

greater blessings for our families

than we can imagine.

He wants the best for them and

for us, as His children.

Because a veil of forgetfulness was placed over our minds at birth, we have had to find a way to RELEARN in this life what we once knew and defended.

Part of our preparation in this life has been to find that precious truth so that we can then RECOMMIT to it by covenant.

To know His will you
must be committed
to do it. The words
"THY WILL BE DONE,"
written in the heart,
are the window to
REVELATION.

What we want with all our **HEARTS** will determine in large degree whether we can claim our right to the companionship of the Holy Ghost, without which there can be no spiritual nourishing.

The Holy Ghost brings back memories of what God has taught us. And one of the ways God teaches us is with His **BLESSINGS**; and so, if we choose to exercise faith, the Holy Ghost will bring God's kindnesses to our **REMEMBRANCE.**

God not only loves

the obedient, He

ENLIGHTENS them.

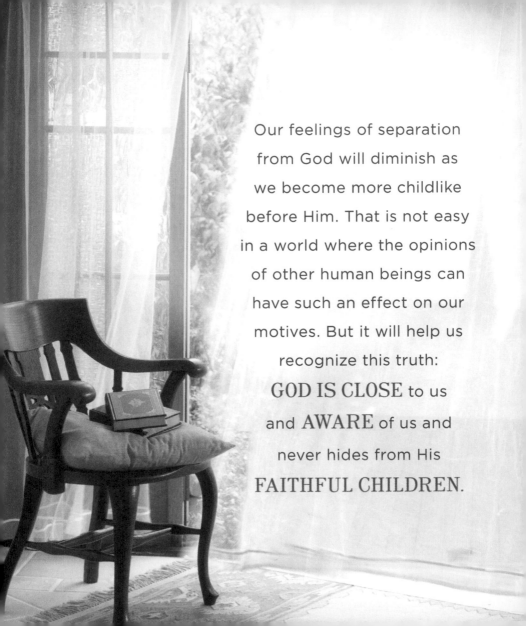

Our feelings of separation from God will diminish as we become more childlike before Him. That is not easy in a world where the opinions of other human beings can have such an effect on our motives. But it will help us recognize this truth: GOD IS CLOSE to us and AWARE of us and never hides from His FAITHFUL CHILDREN.

On many days, doing what
matters most will not be easy.
It is not supposed to be.

God's purpose in
creation was to let us
prove ourselves.

GOD KNOWS OUR GIFTS.

My challenge to you and to me is to pray to know the gifts we have been given, to know how to develop them, and to recognize the opportunities to serve others that God provides us. But most of all, I pray that you will be inspired to help others discover their special gifts from God to serve.

What we will need in our day of testing is a spiritual preparation. It is to have developed faith in Jesus Christ so powerful that we can pass the test of life upon which everything for us in eternity depends. That test is part of the purpose God had for us in the Creation.

The scriptures make the danger of delay clear. It is that we may discover that we have RUN OUT OF TIME. The God who gives us each day as a treasure will require an accounting.

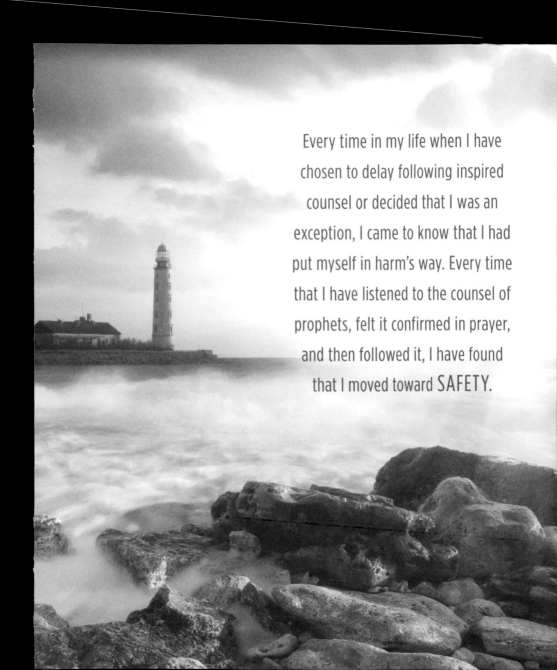

Every time in my life when I have chosen to delay following inspired counsel or decided that I was an exception, I came to know that I had put myself in harm's way. Every time that I have listened to the counsel of prophets, felt it confirmed in prayer, and then followed it, I have found that I moved toward SAFETY.

Words of doctrine [have] great
power. They can open the minds of
people to see SPIRITUAL THINGS
not visible to the natural eye.

And they can OPEN THE HEART
to feelings of the love of God and
a love for truth. The Savior drew on
both those sources of power,
to OPEN OUR EYES
and OPEN HEARTS.

Whatever
our personal
characteristics or
whatever will be our
experiences, there
is but one plan of
HAPPINESS.
That plan is to
follow all the
commandments
of God.

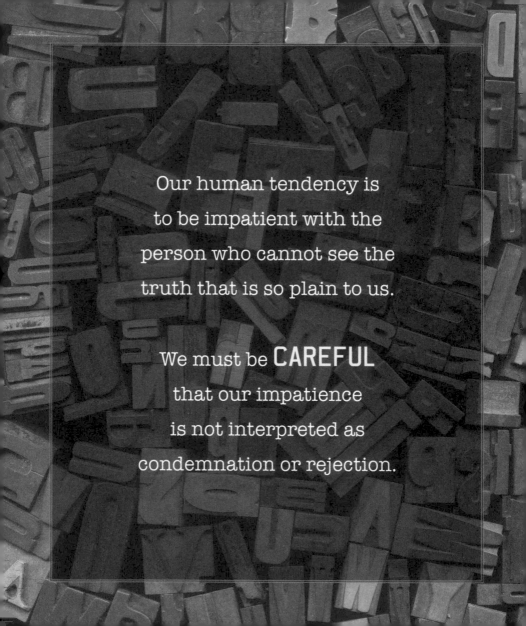

Our human tendency is
to be impatient with the
person who cannot see the
truth that is so plain to us.

We must be **CAREFUL**
that our impatience
is not interpreted as
condemnation or rejection.

WE LIGHTEN THE LOADS

OF OTHERS BEST BY

HELPING THE LORD

STRENGTHEN

THEM.

Our desire to

serve others is

magnified by our

GRATITUDE

for what the Savior

has done for us.

Whether or not you
choose to keep your
covenant to always
remember him,
He always
remembers
.

If we have faith in Jesus Christ,
the hardest as well as the easiest times
in life can be a blessing.

THOSE WHO SUBMIT LIKE A CHILD do it because they know that the Father wants only the **HAPPINESS** of His children and that only He knows the way. That is the testimony we must have to **KEEP PRAYING** like a submissive child, in the good times as well as the times of trouble.

It is never too late to strengthen the foundation of faith. There is always time. With faith in the Savior, you can repent and plead for forgiveness. There is someone you can FORGIVE. There is someone you can THANK. There is someone you can SERVE and LIFT. You can do it wherever you are and however alone and deserted you may feel.

The Lord's great mentors

have shown me that spiritual

staying power comes from

WORKING past the point

when others would have

taken a REST.

There is nothing that has come or will come into your family as important as the

SEALING BLESSINGS.

There is nothing more important than honoring the marriage and family covenants you have made or will make in the temples of God.

The first,
the middle,
and the
last thing
to do is
pray.

THE WAY TO
GROW IN THE
FAITH
THAT WE ARE THE
CHILDREN OF OUR
HEAVENLY FATHER
IS TO ACT LIKE IT.
THE TIME TO
START IS NOW.

This is the Lord's Church.
He called us and trusted us
even in the weaknesses He
knew we had. He knew the
trials we would face. By
faithful service and through His
Atonement, we can come to
WANT WHAT HE WANTS
and BE WHAT WE MUST BE
to bless those we serve for Him.

Don't ignore the impulses that come to you to

RISE ABOVE

yourself into a higher and more beautiful world. Growing up, getting educated, seeing the world, and almost everything that happens to you will push you toward saying to yourself: "Oh, that was just a dream. That's not possible. I could never change that much."

YOU CAN.

The Savior promised: "Come unto me, all ye that labour and are heavy laden, and I will give you rest"

(Matthew 11:28).

JUST AS WE MUST
BE CLEANSED OF SIN
TO HAVE THE SPIRIT
WITH US, WE MUST BE

ENOUGH BEFORE GOD
TO RECOGNIZE OUR
NEED FOR IT.

We never need to feel
that we are alone or
unloved in the Lord's
service because we
never are. We can
feel the love of God.
The Savior has
promised angels
on our left and our
right to bear us up

(see Doctrine and Covenants 84:88).

And He always
keeps His word.

Don't worry
about how
**INEXPERIENCED
YOU ARE,**
or think you are,
but think about
what, with the
Lord's help,
you can
BECOME.

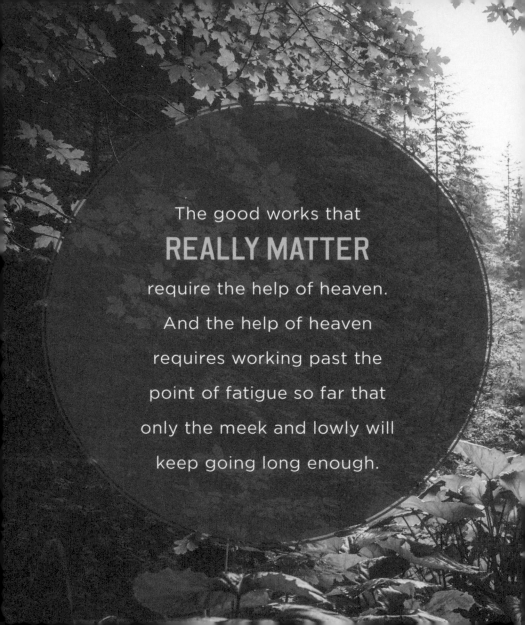

The good works that
REALLY MATTER
require the help of heaven.
And the help of heaven
requires working past the
point of fatigue so far that
only the meek and lowly will
keep going long enough.

Success in the
Lord's service
always produces
MIRACLES
beyond our
own powers.

Have you felt, as I have, the
impression to help someone only
to find that what you were **inspired** to
give was exactly what someone
needed at that **VERY MOMENT?**

That is a wonderful assurance that
God **knows** all of our needs and
counts on us to fill the needs
of others around us.

The Lord doesn't put us through this test just to give us a grade; He does it because the process will **CHANGE US**.

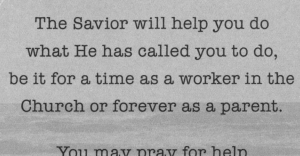

The Savior will help you do
what He has called you to do,
be it for a time as a worker in the
Church or forever as a parent.

You may pray for help
enough to do the work and
KNOW THAT IT WILL COME.

Most people carrying
heavy loads begin
to doubt themselves
and their own worth.
We lighten their loads
as we are PATIENT
with their weaknesses
and CELEBRATE
whatever goodness
we can see in them.
The Lord does that.

You won't always see the **MIRACLES** that come from your work, which is probably a blessing. If you did, you would get proud. But you can often **UNDERESTIMATE** what God is doing as He honors your calling.

Our goal when we teach
our children to pray is for
them to want God to write
upon their **HEARTS** and be
willing then to go and do
what God asks of them.

THE PRETTIEST FLOWERS I've ever seen were among rocks near the tops of mountains. That must have been partly because I worked so hard to get there, for something else. And then, suddenly, there they were. By forcing yourself to look at them, at the BLESSINGS around you, it will be easy to do what King Benjamin suggested: "O how you ought to thank your heavenly King!" (Mosiah 2:19).

If we look for human FRAILTY
in humans, we will always find it.

We live in a world where
finding fault in others seems
to be the favorite blood sport.
It has long been the basis of
political campaign strategy. It
is the theme of much television
programming across the world.
It sells newspapers. Whenever we
meet anyone, our first, almost
unconscious reaction may be to
look for IMPERFECTIONS.

Even the acceptance
of personal responsibility
may not overcome the
temptation to believe
that now is not the
time to repent. "Now"
can seem so difficult,
and "later" appear
so much easier.

The truth is that
TODAY is always a
better day to repent
than any TOMORROW.

When you put the SPIRITUAL THINGS FIRST in your life, you will be blessed to feel directed toward certain learning, and you will be motivated to work harder. You will recognize later that your POWER TO SERVE was increased, and you will be grateful.

You make **CHOICES**
every day and almost
every hour that keep
you walking in the
LIGHT or moving away
toward **DARKNESS.**

You could ask yourself, "How did God bless me today?" If you do that long enough and with faith, you will find yourself remembering **BLESSINGS.** And sometimes you will have gifts brought to your mind which you failed to notice during the day, but which you will then know were a touch of **GOD'S HAND IN YOUR LIFE.**

in GOD, then

GO and DO.

For us to qualify for eternal life, our **SERVICE** in this life must include working with all our heart, might, mind, and strength to prepare others to **RETURN** to God with us.

creates a **NOISE** within us

which makes the **QUIET** voice

of the Spirit hard to hear.

One of the effects of
disobeying God seems to be
the creation of just enough
SPIRITUAL ANESTHETIC to
block any sensation as the
ties to God are being cut.

The covenant promise the Lord made that His disciples could remember His words extends to remembering and recognizing His **BLESSINGS.**

My warning is a simple matter of cause and effect. Jesus Christ is the light and the life of the world. If we do not choose to move **TOWARD** Him, we will find that we have moved **AWAY.**

CHOOSE TO OBEY the Lord quickly,
always, in quiet times and in
storms. As we do, our faith will be
STRENGTHENED, we will find
PEACE in this life, and we will gain
the assurance that we and our families
can qualify for ETERNAL LIFE
in the world to come.

Whatever invites the **HOLY GHOST** to be your companion will bring you greater wisdom and greater ability to obey God.

There are spiritual crops that
require months, years, and
sometimes a lifetime
of cultivation before the
harvest. Among them are

SPIRITUAL REWARDS

you want most.

That shouldn't surprise you.
Common sense tells you
that what matters most
won't come easily.

TIME PASSES

at a fixed rate and
we can't store it. You
can just decide what
to do with it—or not
to do with it.

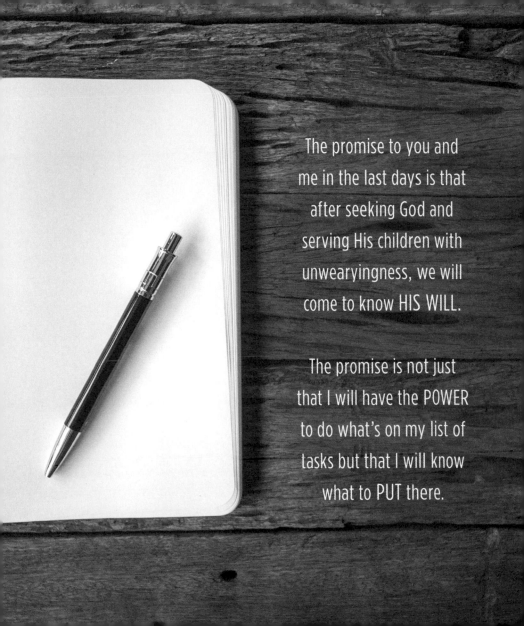

The promise to you and me in the last days is that after seeking God and serving His children with unwearyingness, we will come to know HIS WILL.

The promise is not just that I will have the POWER to do what's on my list of tasks but that I will know what to PUT there.

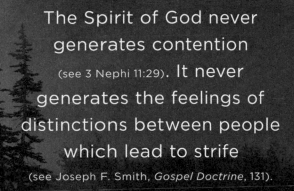

The Spirit of God never
generates contention
(see 3 Nephi 11:29). It never
generates the feelings of
distinctions between people
which lead to strife
(see Joseph F. Smith, *Gospel Doctrine*, 131).

It leads to personal peace and
a feeling of union with others.
IT UNIFIES SOULS.

A man and his wife
learn to be one by using
their similarities to
understand each other
and their differences to
complement each other in
serving one another and
those around them.

One of the sure signs of a
person who has accepted the
gift of the Savior's Atonement
is a willingness to GIVE.

The process of cleansing our
lives seems to make us more
sensitive, more generous,
more pleased to SHARE what
means so much to us.

When we **REACH OUT** to give succor and to lift a burden, He reaches with us. He will lead us to those in need. He will bless us to feel what they feel. As we persist in our efforts to serve them, we will more and more be given the gift of feeling **HIS LOVE** for them.

The IDEAL of doing for each other
what the Lord would have us do,
which follows naturally from
taking His name upon us, can take
us to a spiritual level which is a
TOUCH OF HEAVEN ON EARTH.

THE TRUTH OF MOST WORTH

is to know God our Heavenly Father,
His Son Jesus Christ, and Their
plan for us to have eternal life
with Them in families.

Wherever you live, you have
friends who are SEARCHING
for the greater happiness
you have found in living the
restored gospel of Jesus
Christ. They may not be able
to describe that happiness in
words, but they can recognize it
when they see it in your life.

God will put
prepared people
in the way of His
prepared servants
who want to share
the GOSPEL.

We can take heart that

our honest effort to keep

our covenants allows

God to increase our

POWER to do it.

If you want to receive the

GIFTS OF THE SPIRIT,

you have to want them
for the right reasons. Your
purposes must be the

LORD'S PURPOSES.

To the degree your motives
are selfish, you will find it
difficult to receive those
gifts of the Spirit that have
been promised to you.

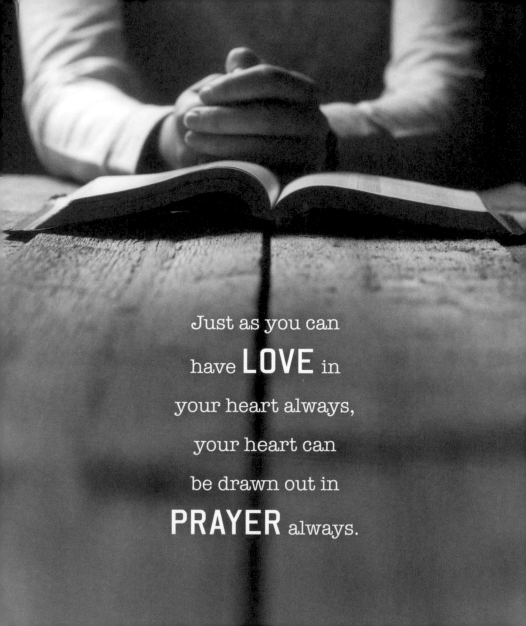

Just as you can have **LOVE** in your heart always, your heart can be drawn out in **PRAYER** always.

I have had PRAYERS answered. Those answers were most clear when what I wanted was silenced by an overpowering need to know what GOD WANTED. It is then that the answer from a loving Heavenly Father can be spoken to the mind by the still, small voice and can be written on the HEART.

At some moment in the world to come, everyone you will ever meet will know what you know now. They will know that the only way to live forever in association with our families and in the presence of our Heavenly Father and His Son, Jesus Christ, was to choose to enter into the gate by BAPTISM at the hands of those with authority from God.

And they will know that YOU KNEW. And they will REMEMBER whether you offered them what someone had offered you.

VIBRANT FAITH in God comes best from **SERVING** Him regularly.

Photo Credits

Page 1: Jag_cz/shutterstock.com

Page 3: Morgan Studio/shutterstock.com

Pages 4–5: filmfullphoto/shutterstock.com

Page 6: PGmart/shutterstock.com

Page 7: threeart/istock

Pages 8–9: 1MoreCreative/istock and Elzbieta Sekowska/shutterstock.com

Page 11: Ulrike Neumann/istock

Pages 12–13: Fototaras/shutterstock.com

Pages 14–15: lucas nishimoto/shutterstock.com

Page 16: marekuliasz/shutterstock.com

Page 17: marekuliasz/shutterstock.com

Pages 18–19: rdonar/shutterstock.com

Page 20: brytta/istock

Pages 22–23: Perfect Lazybones/shutterstock.com

Pages 24–25: pixhook/istock

Pages 26–27: Kichigin/shutterstock.com

Pages 28–29: Andy Nelson/shutterstock.com

Pages 30–31: Nejron Photo/shutterstock.com

Page 32: theskaman306/shutterstock.com

Page 34: Konstanttin/shutterstock.com

Page 35: Christophe Testi/shutterstock.com

Pages 36–37: nueng audok/shutterstock.com

Page 38: Somchai Som/shutterstock.com

Page 39: Dark Moon Pictures/shutterstock.com

Pages 40–41: Kuzma/shutterstock.com

Page 43: Balazs Kovacs/istock

Pages 44–45: Greg Peterson/shutterstock.com

Page 46: Dyna-Mike/istock

Pages 48–49: Shawn Gearhart/istock

Pages 50–51: Paul Aniszewski/shutterstock.com

Page 52: KPG_Payless/shutterstock.com

Pages 54–55: Pachai Leknettip/shutterstock.com

Pages 56–57: eurobanks/istock

Page 59: Gayvoronskaya_Yana/shutterstock.com

Pages 60–61: Sensay/shutterstock.com

Page 63: messkalina/shutterstock.com

Page 64: Kristen Johansen/istock

Pages 66–67: Andrea Carolina Sanchez Gonzalez/istock

Page 68: Adventure_Photo/istock

Page 70: Sunny studio/shutterstock.com

Pages 72–73: PPAMPicture/istock

Pages 74–75: Kichigin/shutterstock.com

Pages 76–77: Ladislav Pavliha

Page 79: Coffee Lover/shutterstock.com

Page 80: Elena Elisseeva/shutterstock.com

Pages 82–83: Galyna Andrushko/shutterstock.com

Page 84: tazytaz/istock

Pages 86–87: Balazs Kovacs/istock

Page 88: HTU/shutterstock.com

Pages 90–91: Nejron Photo/shutterstock.com

Page 92: surasaki/istock

Pages 94–95: BrAt82/shutterstock.com

Pages 96–97: Dubova/shutterstock.com

Page 99: freemixer/istock

Pages 100–101: Standret/shutterstock.com

Page 102: darrya/istock

Pages 104–105: Iri_sha/shutterstock.com

Pages 106–107: Neustockimages/istock

Pages 108–109: Dark Moon Pictures/shutterstock.com

Pages 110–111: Sensay/istock

Page 113: Dark Moon Pictures/shutterstock.com

Pages 114–115: Maica/istock

Page 116: rarrarorro/istock

Pages 118–119: greiss design/shutterstock.com

Page 121: optimarc/shutterstock.com

Page 122: &#169 suzanne clements/istock

Pages 124–125: Rike_/istock

Page 127: muzon/istock

Pages 128–129: Kichigin/shutterstock.com

Page 130: martin951/shutterstock.com

Page 131: Todja/shutterstock.com

Pages 132–133: Galyna Andrushko/shutterstock.com

Pages 134–135: Rike_/istock

Page 137: pikselstock/shutterstock.com

Pages 138–139: Michal Bednarek/shutterstock.com

Page 141: portishead1/istock

Pages 142–143: Monkey Business Images/shutterstock.com

Page 144: Duncan Walker/istock

Page 145: Stokkete/shutterstock.com

Page 147: Galyna Andrushko/shutterstock.com

Pages 148–149: Dawid Andruszkiewicz/istock

Page 150: 4Max/shutterstock.com

Pages 152–153: Suzanne Tucker/shutterstock.com

Pages 154–155: CHOATphotographer/shutterstock.com

Extras: nickfree/istock, Visual Generation/shutterstock.com, abzee/istock, Creativeye99/istock, pashabo/shutterstock.com

All photographs and illustrations throughout the book are used by permission.